# BECOME A REACT 19 POWER DEVELOPER

---

**PRACTICAL PROJECTS AND SOLUTIONS**

OLIVER LUCAS JR

1

# Preface

Welcome to a comprehensive exploration of React 19, a pivotal release that marks a significant evolution in the world's most popular JavaScript library. This book is designed to be your definitive guide, not just to the new features, but to the underlying philosophy and best practices that will empower you to build modern, high-performance web applications.

React 19 isn't merely an incremental update; it represents a paradigm shift. With the introduction of Server Components, React Actions, and the React Compiler, the landscape of React development is being redefined. These advancements are not just about adding new tools; they're about fundamentally changing how we think about building user interfaces, optimizing performance, and managing state.

This book will guide you through the intricacies of React 19, from setting up your development environment to deploying complex applications. We'll dive deep into the core concepts, providing practical examples and in-depth explanations that go beyond surface-level tutorials. Whether you are a seasoned React developer or just beginning your journey, this book will equip you with the knowledge and skills to leverage the full potential of React 19.

We'll start by laying a solid foundation, understanding the key changes and improvements that React 19 brings. You'll learn how to craft reusable components, master advanced JSX techniques, and effectively manage state. We'll then explore the revolutionary features of Server Components and React Actions, delving into their implementation and benefits.

Performance optimization is a cornerstone of this book. We'll cover techniques like code splitting, lazy loading, and memoization, and we'll show you how to identify and resolve performance bottlenecks. You'll also learn how to write effective tests, deploy your applications to production, and maintain code quality and scalability.

This book is more than just a manual; it's a journey into the future of React. We'll explore best practices, discuss real-world scenarios, and provide you with the tools to build robust, scalable, and maintainable applications. By the time you reach the end, you'll not only understand React 19, but you'll be ready to embrace its power and transform your approach to web development.

Thank you for joining me on this exciting journey. Let's build the future of the web, together.

# TABLE OF CONTENTS

## Chapter 6

## Chapter 7

## Chapter 8

## Chapter 9

# Chapter 10

10.1 Writing Effective Unit and Integration Tests with Jest and React Testing Library

10.2 Deploying React 19 Applications to Production Environments

10.3 Maintaining Code Quality and Scalability in React 19 Projects.

# Chapter 1

# React 19: The Foundation and Setup

## 1.1 Introduction to React 19's Core Principles

"React 19 isn't just a version bump; it's a recalibration of how we approach building user interfaces. At its heart, React has always championed a declarative style, where you describe *what* you want the UI to look like, not *how* to change it. This fundamental idea remains, but React 19 refines it, making it even more potent.

Imagine you're building a complex form. In earlier versions, you might have wrestled with manually updating the DOM, managing state transitions, and ensuring consistency. React 19 takes that burden away. You simply declare the form's structure, its input fields, and the desired behavior. React handles the rest, efficiently updating the UI when data changes. This declarative approach, more than ever, lets you focus on the logic of your application, not the minutiae of DOM manipulation.

The component-based architecture, another cornerstone of React, gains new dimensions in React 19. We're not just talking about client-side components anymore. The introduction of server components marks a significant paradigm shift. Picture this: you can now render parts of your application directly on the server, closer to your data source. This means faster initial page loads, improved SEO, and a more seamless user experience. Server components handle data fetching and rendering before sending the HTML to the client, while client components retain their interactive, dynamic nature. This hybrid approach is a game-changer.

One-way data flow, the principle that data moves in a single direction through your application, remains crucial. React 19 leverages this concept to maintain predictability and prevent unintended side effects. When data changes, React efficiently updates the relevant components, ensuring a consistent UI.

React 19 is about more than just new features; it's about refining the core principles that have made React so successful. It's about empowering developers to build high-performance, scalable applications with greater ease and efficiency. This version represents a natural evolution, building upon the foundations of React while embracing the demands of modern web development. You're not just learning a framework; you're learning a mindset, a way of thinking about building interactive experiences. And that mindset, more than ever before, is geared for speed, efficiency, and clarity."

# 1.2 Setting Up Your Development Environment

**1. Installing Node.js:**

**Go to the Node.js website:** Navigate to nodejs.org.

**Download the LTS version:** Look for the "LTS" (Long Term Support) version. This ensures stability and compatibility. Download the installer for your operating system (Windows, macOS, Linux).

**Run the installer:** Follow the on-screen instructions. Accept the default settings unless you have specific requirements.

**Verify the installation:** Open your terminal or command prompt and run `node -v` and `npm -v`. You should see the installed versions of Node.js and npm (Node Package Manager).

**2. Configuring Your Code Editor (VS Code Example):**

**Install VS Code:** If you haven't already, download and install VS Code from code.visualstudio.com.

**Install essential extensions:**

**ESLint:** Helps you catch syntax errors and enforce code style. Search for "ESLint" in the VS Code extensions marketplace and install it.

**Prettier:** Formats your code for consistency. Search for "Prettier - Code formatter" and install it.

**React Developer Tools:** Useful for debugging React applications. Search for "React Developer Tools" and install it.

**JavaScript (ES6) code snippets:** Provides code snippets for faster development. Search for "JavaScript (ES6) code snippets" and install it.

**Configure ESLint and Prettier:**

Create `.eslintrc.json` and `.prettierrc.json` files in your project root.

Configure them according to your preferred coding style. Example `.eslintrc.json` <!-- end list →

JSON

```
{
  "extends": ["eslint:recommended", "plugin:react/recommended"],
  "parserOptions": {
    "ecmaVersion": 2023,
    "sourceType": "module",
    "ecmaFeatures": {
      "jsx": true
    }
  },
  "plugins": ["react"],
  "rules": {
```

```
    "react/prop-types": "off"
  },
  "settings": {
    "react": {
      "version": "detect"
    }
  }
}
```

Example `.prettierrc.json`

JSON

```json
{
  "semi": true,
  "trailingComma": "all",
  "singleQuote": true,
  "printWidth": 120,
  "tabWidth": 2
}
```

## 3. Setting Up a React 19 Project with Vite:

**Create a new Vite project:** Open your terminal and run:

Bash

```bash
npm create vite@latest my-react-app --template react
cd my-react-app
```

**Install dependencies:** Run `npm install`.

**Start the development server:** Run `npm run dev`. This will start the Vite development server and open your application in your browser.

**Project Structure:** Explain the basic project structure that vite creates, like the public folder, src folder, and the package.json file.

## 4. Version Control with Git:

**Initialize a Git repository:** In your project directory, run `git init`.

**Create a `.gitignore` file:** Add files and directories that you don't want to track (e.g., `node_modules`).

**Make your first commit:**

Bash

```
git add .
git commit -m "Initial commit"
```

## 5. Browser Developer Tools:

**Open developer tools:** In your browser, press F12 (or right-click and select "Inspect").

**Explore the Elements, Console, and Network tabs:** Familiarize yourself with these tabs, which will be essential for debugging and performance analysis.

**Install the React Developer tools browser extension:** This enables you to inspect react components in the browser.

By following these steps, you'll have a fully functional React 19 development environment ready to go. This hands-on approach will empower you to start building your own React 19 applications with confidence."

# 1.3 Understanding the Key Changes and Improvements

"React 19 isn't just a minor update; it's a strategic evolution designed to address the challenges of modern web development. To truly leverage its power, we need to go beyond surface-level descriptions and understand the 'why' behind each change.

### 1. Server Components: The Paradigm Shift

### Beyond Client-Side Rendering:

We'll begin by exploring the limitations of traditional client-side rendering (CSR). How it impacts initial load times, SEO, and overall performance.

We'll then dive deep into how server components solve these issues by rendering parts of the UI on the server, closer to the data source.

This isn't just about moving code; it's about shifting the mental model of how we build applications.

We will explain the network impact of server components, and how they reduce the amount of javascript sent to the client.

### Data Fetching and Caching:

We'll examine how server components simplify data fetching, allowing you to directly access data sources without complex API calls.

We'll discuss how React 19 leverages server-side caching to optimize data retrieval and reduce database load.

We will explain the security implications of server components.

**Progressive Enhancement**

Explain how server components enhance the user experience, by sending down already rendered HTML.

## 2. React Actions: Streamlining Data Mutations

**Simplified Form Handling:**

We'll dissect how React Actions simplify form handling, eliminating the need for manual event handlers and state updates.

We'll explore how actions handle data mutations, error handling, and user feedback in a declarative and efficient manner.

We will explain how to use actions with server components.

**Asynchronous Operations:**

We'll delve into how actions handle asynchronous operations, such as API calls and database updates, without blocking the UI.

We'll discuss how actions provide built-in mechanisms for managing loading states and handling errors.

We will explain how to use actions to handle optimistic updates.

**Security Considerations:**

Explain how react actions can help mitigate security risks.

## 3. Enhanced Hooks and Performance Optimizations

**useMemo and useCallback Refinements:**

We'll go beyond basic usage and explore advanced techniques for optimizing performance with `useMemo` and `useCallback`.

We'll discuss how React 19 optimizes these hooks to reduce unnecessary re-renders.

We will explain how to use the react dev tools to analyze hook performance.

## New Hooks and APIs

We will explain any new hooks or api's that are introduced in react 19.

Explain how the new hooks or api's improve developer experience.

## Automatic Batching and Transitions:

Explain how React 19 improves automatic batching.

Explain how the transition api works, and how it improves user experience.

## 4. React Compiler

Explain how the react compiler will optimize react code.

Explain the benefits of the react compiler.

Explain the current state of the react compiler.

## 5. Accessibility Improvements:

Explain any accessibility improvements that are included in react 19.

Explain why these improvements are important.

Understanding these changes isn't just about memorizing a list; it's about grasping the underlying principles that drive React 19's evolution. By understanding the 'why,' you'll be able to leverage these improvements to build more performant, scalable, and user-friendly applications."

# Chapter 2

# Mastering React 19 Components and JSX

## 2.1 Building Reusable Components with Functional and Class Components

"Components are the building blocks of any React application. Their reusability is paramount for maintaining a clean, efficient, and scalable codebase. In React 19, we'll delve into the intricacies of crafting these components using both functional and class approaches.

### 1. Functional Components: The Modern Standard

**The Power of Simplicity:**

Functional components, with their concise syntax, promote a declarative style

JavaScript

```javascript
function Greeting({ name }) {
  return <h1>Hello, {name}!</h1>;
}
```

**Leveraging Hooks for State and Side Effects:**

Managing state with useState:

JavaScript

```javascript
import React, { useState } from 'react';
```

```
function Counter() {
  const [count, setCount] = useState(0);

  return (
    <div>
      <p>Count: {count}</p>
              <button  onClick={()  =>  setCount(count  +
1)}>Increment</button>
    </div>
  );
}
```

Using useReducer for complex state

JavaScript

```
import React, { useReducer } from 'react';

const initialState = { count: 0 };

function reducer(state, action) {
  switch (action.type) {
    case 'increment':
      return { count: state.count + 1 };
    case 'decrement':
      return { count: state.count - 1 };
    default:
      throw new Error();
  }
}

function ComplexCounter() {
  const [state, dispatch] = useReducer(reducer, initialState);
```

```
  return (
    <div>
      <p>Count: {state.count}</p>
            <button onClick={() => dispatch({ type: 'increment'
})}>Increment</button>
            <button onClick={() => dispatch({ type: 'decrement'
})}>Decrement</button>
    </div>
  );
}
```

**Composition[1] and Reusability Patterns:**
Render props:

JavaScript

```
function MouseTracker({ render }) {
  const [mousePosition, setMousePosition] = useState({ x: 0, y: 0
});

  const handleMouseMove = (event) => {
    setMousePosition({ x: event.clientX, y: event.clientY });
  };

  return (
    <div onMouseMove={handleMouseMove}>
      {render(mousePosition)}
    </div>
  );
}

function App() {
  return (
    <MouseTracker
      render={(({ x, y }) => (
```

```
      <p>Mouse position: ({x}, {y})</p>
    )}
  />
);
}
```

## 2. Class Components: Understanding the Legacy

## The Component Lifecycle

JavaScript

```
import React from 'react';

class LifecycleExample extends React.Component {
  constructor(props) {
    super(props);
    this.state = { count: 0 };
    console.log('Constructor called');
  }

  componentDidMount() {
    console.log('Component did mount');
    document.title = `Count: ${this.state.count}`;
  }

  componentDidUpdate(prevProps, prevState) {
    console.log('Component did update');
    if (prevState.count !== this.state.count) {
      document.title = `Count: ${this.state.count}`;
    }
  }

  componentWillUnmount() {
    console.log('Component will unmount');
  }
```

```
  render() {
    console.log('Render called');
    return (
      <div>
        <p>Count: {this.state.count}</p>
        <button onClick={() => this.setState({ count: this.state.count +
1 })}>
        Increment
        </button>
      </div>
    );
  }
}
```

**Refactoring Class Components to Functional Components:**

JavaScript

```
// Original Class Component
class GreetingClass extends React.Component {
  render() {
    return <h1>Hello, {this.props.name}!</h1>;
  }
}

// Refactored Functional Component
function GreetingFunction({ name }) {
  return <h1>Hello, {name}!</h1>;
}
```

### 3. Best Practices for Component Reusability

**Component Design Principles**

Single responsibility principle: each component should have one job

**Naming Conventions and Folder Structure:**

Example folder structure:

```
src/
  components/
    Button/
      Button.jsx
      Button.module.css
      Button.test.jsx
    Card/
      Card.jsx
      Card.module.css
      Card.test.jsx
```

By integrating these coding examples, we provide a more hands-on and practical understanding of building reusable components in React 19."

## 2.2 Advanced JSX Techniques and Best Practices: Crafting Elegant UIs

"JSX, the syntactic sugar that allows us to write HTML-like structures within JavaScript, is a powerful tool in React. However, to truly harness its potential, we need to go beyond the basics and explore advanced techniques and best practices.

### 1. Conditional Rendering: Beyond Simple If Statements

**Ternary Operators and Logical AND**

We'll explore how to use ternary operators and logical AND (&&) for concise conditional rendering.

JavaScript

```
function StatusMessage({ isLoggedIn }) {
  return (
    <div>
      {isLoggedIn ? <p>Welcome back!</p> : <p>Please log in.</p>}
      {isLoggedIn && <p>You have unread messages.</p>}
    </div>
  );
}
```

We will explain how to prevent rendering when a condition is false.

**Short-Circuit Evaluation and Fragment Usage:**

We'll discuss how short-circuit evaluation can simplify conditional rendering and how fragments (<> ... </>) can be used to group elements without adding extra DOM nodes.

JavaScript

```
function OptionalComponent({ show }) {
  return (
    <>
      {show && <p>This component is conditionally rendered.</p>}
      <p>This component is always rendered.</p>
    </>
  );
}
```

Explain how to return null, when you do not want to render anything.

## Using components to handle complex conditional logic.

Explain how to create a component that will handle the complex logic, and return the correct JSX.

## 2. List Rendering: Efficiently Displaying Collections

### Using `map()` with Keys:

We'll emphasize the importance of using unique key props when rendering lists with `map()`.

JavaScript

```
function ItemList({ items }) {
  return (
    <ul>
     {items.map((item) => (
       <li key={item.id}>{item.name}</li>
     ))}
    </ul>
  );
}
```

Explain why keys are important for performance.

### Fragments and Keyed Fragments

We'll explore how to use fragments and keyed fragments (`<React.Fragment key={...}>`) when rendering complex lists.

Explain how to use index as a key, and when it is appropriate.

**Handling Empty Lists and Loading States:**

Explain how to display a message when a list is empty.

Explain how to display a loading state, while a list is being fetched.

**3. Composition and Abstraction: Creating Reusable Patterns**

**Component Composition with `children`:**

We'll delve into how to use the `children` prop to create flexible and reusable components.

JavaScript

```javascript
function Card({ children }) {
  return <div className="card">{children}</div>;
}

function App() {
  return (
    <Card>
      <h2>Card Title</h2>
      <p>Card content goes here.</p>
    </Card>
  );
}
```

Explain how to use named slots, rather than just children.

**Creating Custom JSX Elements:**

Explain how to create custom components that behave like standard html elements.

**Abstracting Repetitive Patterns:**

Explain how to create components that abstract away repetitive patterns.

## 4. JSX Best Practices: Writing Clean and Maintainable Code

**Using Descriptive Variable Names:**

We'll emphasize the importance of using descriptive variable names to enhance code readability

**Breaking Down Complex JSX:**

We'll discuss how to break down complex JSX structures into smaller, more manageable components.

**Consistent Formatting and Indentation:**

We'll highlight the importance of consistent formatting and indentation for code maintainability.

Explain how to use prettier to enforce consistent formatting.

**Avoiding Inline Styles (When Possible):**

Explain the benefits of CSS modules, or styled components.

Explain when inline styles are appropriate.

By mastering these advanced JSX techniques and best practices, you'll be able to create elegant, efficient, and maintainable user interfaces in your React 19 applications."

## 2.3 Component Lifecycle and State Management Basics

"Understanding the component lifecycle and mastering state management are crucial for building dynamic and interactive React applications. In this section, we'll cover the basics, laying a solid foundation for more advanced concepts.

### 1. Component Lifecycle: The Stages of a Component's Life

**Mounting: Bringing Components to Life:**

We'll begin by exploring the mounting phase, where components are created and inserted into the DOM.

We'll focus on the constructor (for class components), and how functional components are initialized.

Explain how the initial render happens.

**Updating: Reacting to Changes:**

We'll delve into the updating phase, where components re-render in response to changes in props or state.

We'll discuss how React determines when to re-render, and how to optimize re-renders.

Explain how react 19 improves upon previous re-rendering methods.

**Unmounting: Saying Goodbye:**

We'll cover the unmounting phase, where components are removed from the DOM.

We'll emphasize the importance of cleaning up resources, such as event listeners or timers, to prevent memory leaks.

Explain how to use the return function inside of useEffect to handle unmounting.

**Error Handling:**

Explain how to use the error boundaries to handle errors inside of components.

Explain how to use try catch blocks inside of components.

## 2. State Management: The Heart of Dynamic UIs

**Local State: Managing Component-Specific Data:**

We'll start with local state, which allows components to manage their own data

We'll demonstrate how to use `useState` in functional components to manage state variables.

Explain how to update state correctly.

Explain how to use the useState setter function.

**Props: Passing Data Down the Component Tree:**

We'll explore how props are used to pass data from parent to child components.

We'll emphasize the importance of immutability and data flow.

Explain how to use prop-types, or typescript, to validate props.

**State Updates and Re-renders:**

We'll discuss how state updates trigger re-renders, and how React efficiently updates the DOM.

Explain how React batches state updates.

Explain how to force a re-render.

**Immutable State:**

Explain why immutable state is important.

Explain how to update state immutably.

Explain how to use libraries like Immer to help with immutable state.

### 3. Best Practices for State Management

### Keeping State Minimal:

We'll emphasize the importance of keeping state minimal and avoiding unnecessary state variables.

### Lifting State Up:

We'll discuss how to lift state up to a common ancestor component when multiple components need access to the same data.

### Using Context API for Shared State:

Explain how to use the context API for sharing state between components.

### State Management Libraries:

Briefly explain the use cases for state management libraries, like redux, or zustand.

By understanding these fundamentals, you'll be well-equipped to build robust and interactive React 19 applications."

# Chapter 3

# React 19 Hooks: The Power of Functionality

## 3.1 Deep Dive into Essential Hooks (useState, useEffect, useContext)

"Hooks are the cornerstone of modern React development, allowing us to leverage state and lifecycle features within functional components. In this section, we'll go beyond basic usage and explore the intricacies of useState, useEffect, and useContext.

### 1. useState: Beyond Simple State Variables

**Complex State Updates:**

We'll explore how to use useState with complex data structures like objects and arrays, emphasizing the importance of immutability.

We'll discuss how to use the functional update form of useState to avoid stale closures and ensure accurate state updates.

Example:

JavaScript

```
const [items, setItems] = useState([]);

const addItem = (newItem) => {
  setItems((prevItems) => [...prevItems, newItem]);
}
```

**Lazy Initialization:**

We'll demonstrate how to use lazy initialization to compute the initial state only once, improving performance.
Example

JavaScript

```javascript
const [expensiveData, setExpensiveData] = useState(() => {
  // Perform expensive computation here
  return computeInitialData();
});
```

**State Co-location:**

Explain how to colocate state, when it makes sense to do so.

**2. useEffect: Mastering Side Effects**

**Cleanup Functions: Preventing Memory Leaks:**

We'll emphasize the importance of cleanup functions to prevent memory leaks and ensure proper resource management.

We'll provide examples of how to clean up event listeners, timers, and subscriptions.

Example:

JavaScript

```javascript
useEffect(() => {
  const timerId = setInterval(() => {
    console.log('Tick');
  }, 1000);

  return () => {
    clearInterval(timerId);
  };
```

```
}, []);
```

## Dependency Arrays: Optimizing Performance:

We'll delve into the nuances of dependency arrays, explaining how to use them to control when `useEffect` runs.

We'll discuss how to use empty dependency arrays ( [ ] ) for mount and unmount effects, and how to specify dependencies for update effects.

Explain how to use the dependency array to correctly handle callbacks.

## Fetching Data and Handling Loading States:

Explain how to use useEffect to fetch data from an API.

Explain how to handle loading states, and error states, while fetching data.

## 3. useContext: Sharing Data Across the Component Tree

## Creating and Consuming Contexts:

We'll demonstrate how to create contexts with `createContext` and consume them with `useContext`.

We'll explain how to use context providers to share data across the component tree.

Example:

JavaScript

```javascript
import React, { createContext, useContext, useState } from 'react';
```

```
const ThemeContext = createContext();

function ThemeProvider({ children }) {
  const [theme, setTheme] = useState('light');

  return (
    <ThemeContext.Provider value={{ theme, setTheme }}>
      {children}
    </ThemeContext.Provider>
  );
}

function ThemedComponent() {
  const { theme, setTheme } = useContext(ThemeContext);

  return (
    <div style={{ background: theme === 'light' ? '#fff' : '#333', color:
theme === 'light' ? '#000' : '#fff' }}>
      <p>Current theme: {theme}</p>
        <button onClick={() => setTheme(theme === 'light' ? 'dark' :
'light')}>Toggle theme</button>
    </div>
  );
}
```

**Context Performance Considerations:**

We'll discuss how context updates can trigger re-renders in consuming components and how to optimize performance.

Explain how to use memoization with context.

**Combining Context with useReducer:**
Explain how to use context to pass down a dispatch function, from a useReducer.

By mastering these essential hooks, you'll be able to build powerful and efficient functional components in React 19."

# 3.2 Creating Custom Hooks for Reusable Logic

"Custom hooks are a powerful way to encapsulate and reuse logic across your React 19 components. They allow you to extract stateful logic and side effects into reusable functions, promoting cleaner and more maintainable code.

## 1. Identifying Reusable Logic:

**Recognizing Patterns:**

We'll start by exploring how to identify common patterns in your components that can be extracted into custom hooks.

This includes logic for data fetching, form handling, event listeners, and state management.

We'll discuss how to recognize when a piece of logic is becoming too complex or repetitive.

**Encapsulating Side Effects:**

We'll emphasize how custom hooks can encapsulate side effects, such as API calls or DOM manipulations, making them easier to manage and test.

Explain how to create a custom hook, that handles subscribing and unsubscribing to events.

## 2. Building Custom Hooks: A Step-by-Step Guide:

### Naming Conventions:

We'll emphasize the importance of following the use prefix for custom hook names, making them easily recognizable.

Explain how to name custom hooks, to make them easy to understand.

### Extracting State and Side Effects:

We'll demonstrate how to extract state variables and side effects from components into custom hooks.

We'll provide examples of how to use useState, useEffect, and useContext within custom hooks.

Example:

JavaScript

```javascript
import { useState, useEffect } from 'react';

function useFetch(url) {
  const [data, setData] = useState(null);
  const [loading, setLoading] = useState(true);
  const [error, setError] = useState(null);

  useEffect(() => {
    const fetchData = async () => {
      try {
        const response = await fetch(url);
        if (!response.ok) {
          throw new Error(`HTTP error! status: ${response.status}`);
        }
        const result = await response.json();
```

```
      setData(result);
    } catch (err) {
      setError(err);
    } finally {
      setLoading(false);
    }
  };

  fetchData();
}, [url]);

  return { data, loading, error };
}
```

## Returning Values and Functions:

We'll discuss how to return values and functions from custom hooks, allowing components to interact with the encapsulated logic.

Explain how to return a dispatch function, from a useReducer.

## 3. Best Practices for Custom Hooks:

## Keeping Hooks Focused:

We'll emphasize the importance of keeping custom hooks focused on a single responsibility.

This promotes reusability and maintainability.

## Testing Custom Hooks:

We'll explore how to write unit tests for custom hooks, ensuring their correctness and reliability.

Explain how to test hooks, that use side effects.

**Composing Custom Hooks:**

We'll discuss how to compose custom hooks to create more complex and powerful logic.

Explain how to use one custom hook, inside of another.

**Documenting Custom Hooks:**

Explain the importance of documenting custom hooks.

Explain how to properly document custom hooks.

By mastering the creation of custom hooks, you'll be able to significantly enhance the reusability and maintainability of your React 19 applications."

# 3.3 Optimizing Performance with useMemo and useCallback

"Performance optimization is crucial for creating smooth and responsive React 19 applications. `useMemo` and `useCallback` are powerful hooks that allow us to memoize expensive computations and prevent unnecessary re-renders.

**1. Understanding Memoization:**

**The Concept of Memoization:**

We'll begin by explaining the concept of memoization, which involves caching the results of expensive function calls and returning the cached result when the same inputs occur again.[1]

We'll discuss how memoization can improve performance by avoiding redundant computations.

**When to Use Memoization:**

We'll explore the scenarios where memoization is most beneficial, such as:

Expensive computations that are performed on every render.

Rendering components that receive complex or frequently changing props.

Passing callback functions to child components.

**2. useMemo: Memoizing Computed Values:**

**Basic Usage**

We'll demonstrate how to use useMemo to memoize the results of expensive computations.

Example:

JavaScript

```javascript
import React, { useMemo } from 'react';

function ExpensiveCalculation({ a, b }) {
  const result = useMemo(() => {
    console.log('Calculating...');
    let sum = 0;
    for (let i = 0; i < 100000000; i++) {
      sum += a + b;
    }
    return sum;
  }, [a, b]);

  return <p>Result: {result}</p>;
}
```

Explain how the dependency array controls when the memoized value is recalculated.

**Memoizing Complex Objects and Arrays:**

We'll discuss how to use useMemo to memoize complex objects and arrays, preventing unnecessary re-renders when their values haven't changed.

Explain how to use deep comparison functions, when needed.

**Performance Considerations:**

We'll emphasize the importance of using useMemo judiciously, as it adds overhead.

Explain how to use the react dev tools, to see if useMemo is actually improving performance.

**3. useCallback: Memoizing Callback Functions:**

**Basic Usage:**

We'll demonstrate how to use useCallback to memoize callback functions, preventing unnecessary re-renders in child components.

Example:

JavaScript

```javascript
import React, { useCallback } from 'react';

function Button({ onClick, children }) {
  return <button onClick={onClick}>{children}</button>;
}
```

```
function ParentComponent({ a, b }) {
  const handleClick = useCallback(() => {
    console.log('Button clicked');
    // Perform some action here
  }, [a, b]);

  return <Button onClick={handleClick}>Click me</Button>;
}
```

Explain how the dependency array controls when the memoized callback is recreated.

**Passing Memoized Callbacks to Child Components:**

We'll discuss how to pass memoized callbacks to child components, preventing them from re-rendering when the parent component re-renders.

**Using useCallback with useEffect:**

Explain how to use useCallback to memoize functions that are used inside of useEffect.

**4. Best Practices for Memoization:**

**Profiling and Measuring Performance**

We'll emphasize the importance of profiling and measuring performance before and after applying memoization.

Explain how to use the performance tab in the browser dev tools.

**Avoiding Premature Optimization:**

We'll caution against premature optimization, as it can lead to unnecessary complexity and overhead.

## Understanding Dependency Arrays

We'll emphasize the importance of correctly specifying dependency arrays for useMemo and useCallback.

Explain the dangers of incorrect dependency arrays.

By mastering useMemo and useCallback, you'll be able to significantly enhance the performance of your React 19 applications, creating smooth and responsive user experiences."

# Chapter 4

# React 19 Server Components: A New Paradigm

## 4.1 Understanding Server Components and Their Benefits

"Server components represent a fundamental shift in how we build React applications. They allow us to render parts of our UI on the server, unlocking significant performance and developer experience improvements. To fully leverage their power, it's crucial to understand their inner workings and the benefits they offer.

### 1. The Concept of Server Components:

### Beyond Client-Side Rendering:

We'll start by revisiting the limitations of traditional client-side rendering (CSR), such as increased initial load times and poor SEO.

We'll then introduce the concept of server components, explaining how they enable server-side rendering (SSR) for specific parts of the UI.

Explain how Server components are rendered on the server, and the resulting html is sent to the client.

### Data Fetching on the Server:

We'll discuss how server components allow us to fetch data directly from data sources on the server, eliminating the need for client-side API calls.

Explain how this reduces network latency and improves data security.

Explain how to fetch data from databases, and file systems, directly from server components.

**Zero Client-Side JavaScript:**

Explain how server components can return JSX that contains no client side javascript.

Explain how this drastically reduces the size of the javascript bundle.

**2. Benefits of Server Components:**

**Improved Initial Load Times:**

We'll demonstrate how server components can significantly reduce initial load times by delivering pre-rendered HTML to the client.

Explain how this leads to a faster and more responsive user experience.

**Enhanced SEO:**

We'll discuss how server components improve SEO by making content readily available to search engine crawlers.

Explain how search engines can index the content of server components.

**Reduced Client-Side Bundle Size:**

We'll explain how server components reduce the size of the client-side JavaScript bundle by moving data fetching and rendering logic to the server

Explain how this leads to faster page loads and improved performance on low-powered devices.

### Simplified Data Fetching:

We'll demonstrate how server components simplify data fetching by allowing direct access to data sources on the server.

Explain how this eliminates the need for complex client-side data fetching logic.

### Improved Security:

Because sensitive data access happens on the server, and not the client, explain how this increases security.

Explain how server components can prevent exposing api keys, and database credentials to the client.

### 3. Server Components and Client Components:

### The Hybrid Approach:

We'll emphasize that server components are not a replacement for client components; rather, they complement each other.

Explain how to use both server components, and client components, in the same react application.

Explain the rules for how server and client components can interact with each other.

### When to Use Server Components:

We'll provide guidance on when to use server components, such as for data-heavy pages, static content, and server-side logic.

Explain when to use client components, such as for interactive elements, and client side state.

By understanding the concept and benefits of server components, you'll be able to leverage their power to build high-performance and user-friendly React 19 applications."

## 4.2 Implementing Server Components in Your Applications

"Understanding the theory behind server components is essential, but putting them into practice is where the real power lies. In this section, we'll walk through the steps of implementing server components in your React 19 applications.

### 1. Setting Up Your Project

**Project Requirements:**

We'll outline the necessary project setup, including Node.js version and React 19 configuration.

Explain the differences in project setup between a standard react project, and a project that uses server components.

**Creating Server Components:**

We'll demonstrate how to create server components by using the `.server.js` or `.server.jsx` file extension.

Explain the limitations of server components, such as not being able to use client side hooks.

Example:

JavaScript

```
// ProductList.server.jsx
async function getProducts() {
  // Fetch products from a database or API
```

```
  const response = await fetch('https://api.example.com/products');
  return response.json();
}

export default async function ProductList() {
  const products = await getProducts();

  return (
    <ul>
      {products.map((product) => (
        <li key={product.id}>{product.name}</li>
      ))}
    </ul>
  );
}
```

## 2. Data Fetching in Server Components

### Direct Data Access:

We'll demonstrate how to fetch data directly from data sources, such as databases or APIs, within server components.

Explain how to use async/await to handle asynchronous data fetching.

Explain how to handle errors during data fetching.

### Caching Data:

We'll discuss how to implement server-side caching to optimize data retrieval and reduce database load.

Explain how to cache api responses.

## 3. Integrating Server Components with Client Components:

### The Client Boundary:

We'll explain how to create client boundaries using the `use client` directive, separating server components from client components.

Explain how to pass data from server components, to client components.

Example:

JavaScript

```javascript
// InteractiveButton.client.jsx
'use client';

import { useState } from 'react';

export default function InteractiveButton({ initialCount }) {
  const [count, setCount] = useState(initialCount);

  return (
    <button onClick={() => setCount(count + 1)}>
      Clicked {count} times
    </button>
  );
}
```

### Passing Data from Server to Client:

Explain how to serialize data, and pass it from server components, to client components.

Explain the limitations of what data can be passed.

## 4. Rendering and Deployment:

### Server-Side Rendering Process:

We'll walk through the server-side rendering process, explaining how React generates HTML from server components.

Explain how the server sends the html, and the client side javascript, to the browser.

### Deployment Considerations:

We'll discuss deployment considerations for applications using server components, such as server requirements and build processes.

Explain how to deploy server components to different hosting providers.

Explain how to configure your build process, to handle server components.

## 5. Practical Examples:

### Building a Data-Driven Page:

We'll provide a practical example of building a data-driven page using server components, showcasing data fetching and rendering.

### Creating a Static Content Page:

We'll demonstrate how to use server components to create static content pages, improving SEO and performance.

By following these steps and examples, you'll be able to confidently implement server components in your React 19 applications, unlocking their performance and developer experience benefits."

## 4.3 Data Fetching and Rendering Strategies with Server Components

"Server components revolutionize how we handle data fetching and rendering in React 19. To fully leverage their potential, we need to understand the various strategies and techniques for optimizing server-side interactions.

### 1. Data Fetching Strategies

**Direct Database Access:**

We'll explore how server components enable direct access to databases, eliminating the need for intermediary APIs.

Explain how to use database drivers directly in server components.

Explain how to handle database connections, and connection pooling.

Example:

JavaScript

```
// ProductList.server.jsx
import { getProductsFromDatabase } from './database';

export default async function ProductList() {
  const products = await getProductsFromDatabase();

  return (
    <ul>
      {products.map((product) => (
```

```
      <li key={product.id}>{product.name}</li>
    ))}
  </ul>
  );
}
```

## API Integration

We'll discuss how to integrate with external APIs within server components, fetching data directly from remote sources.

Explain how to handle API authentication, and authorization.

Explain how to handle API rate limiting

Explain how to use environment variables to store api keys.

## File System Access:

Explain how server components can read data directly from the file system.

Explain use cases, such as reading markdown files, or configuration files

## Caching Strategies:

We'll delve into various caching strategies for server components, including:
In-memory caching
Database caching
CDN caching

Explain how to use caching headers.

Explain how to invalidate the cache.

## 2. Rendering Strategies:

### Streaming Rendering:

We'll explore how React 19's streaming rendering capabilities enhance the user experience by progressively delivering HTML to the client.

Explain how streaming rendering improves perceived performance.

Explain how to handle loading states during streaming rendering.

### Partial Hydration:

We'll discuss how server components enable partial hydration, allowing us to selectively hydrate interactive components on the client.

Explain how partial hydration reduces client side javascript.

Explain how to use the use client directive to control hydration.

### Static Site Generation (SSG) with Server Components

Explain how to use server components to generate static sites.

Explain the benefits of static site generation, such as improved performance, and SEO.

Explain how to generate static pages at build time.

## Dynamic Server Rendering

Explain how to use server components to render dynamic content, based on user requests.

Explain how to handle user authentication, and authorization, during dynamic server rendering.

## 3. Optimizing Data Fetching and Rendering:

### Data Colocation:

We'll emphasize the importance of colocating data fetching logic with the components that use it.

Explain how data colocation improves code organization.

### Efficient Data Serialization:

We'll discuss how to optimize data serialization for efficient transmission between the server and client

Explain how to use JSON.stringify, and JSON.parse, efficiently.

Explain how to use libraries like Protobuf.

### Performance Monitoring:

Explain how to monitor the performance of server components, using server side logging, and performance monitoring tools.

Explain how to use the performance tab in the browser dev tools, to analyze client side performance.

### Error Handling

Explain how to properly handle errors during data fetching, and rendering, on the server

Explain how to log errors.

Explain how to display error messages to the user.

By mastering these data fetching and rendering strategies, you'll be able to build highly performant and user-friendly React 19 applications with server components."

# Chapter 5

# React 19 Actions and Data Mutations

## 5.1 Form Handling and Data Submission with React Actions.

"React Actions introduce a powerful and declarative way to handle form submissions and data mutations in React 19. They simplify the process of interacting with server-side logic, enhancing both developer experience and application performance.

### 1. Understanding React Actions:

### Declarative Data Mutations:

We'll start by explaining how React Actions provide a declarative approach to data mutations, allowing you to define the desired outcome without worrying about the implementation details.

Explain how actions are functions that are passed to form elements.

Explain how actions can be asynchronous.

### Server-Side Integration:

We'll discuss how React Actions seamlessly integrate with server components, enabling direct communication with server-side logic.

Explain how actions can be used to directly interact with databases, and apis

**Progressive Enhancement:**

Explain how react actions can be used to progressively enhance forms.

**2. Implementing Form Handling with React Actions:**

**Creating Actions:**

We'll demonstrate how to create React Actions using asynchronous functions.

Example:

JavaScript

```javascript
// SubmitForm.server.jsx
'use server';

export async function submitForm(formData) {
  const name = formData.get('name');
  const email = formData.get('email');

  // Process the form data on the server
  console.log('Form data:', { name, email });

  // Example: Save data to database
  // await saveToDatabase({ name, email });

  return { message: 'Form submitted successfully!' };
}

export default function SubmitForm() {
  return (
    <form action={submitForm}>
      <input type="text" name="name" placeholder="Name" />
      <input type="email" name="email" placeholder="Email" />
```

```
      <button type="submit">Submit</button>
    </form>
  );
}
```

Explain how to access form data.

Explain how to handle errors inside of actions.

**Using Actions with Forms:**

We'll demonstrate how to associate React Actions with form elements using the `action` prop.

Explain how react handles the form submission, and sends the data to the action.

**Handling Success and Error States:**

Explain how to handle success and error states in actions.

Explain how to return data from actions, and how to use that data in the client.

Example:

JavaScript

```
// SubmitForm.client.jsx
'use client';

import { useState, useTransition } from 'react';
import SubmitFormServer, { submitForm } from './SubmitForm.server';
```

```
export default function SubmitFormClient() {
  const [message, setMessage] = useState(null);
  const [pending, startTransition] = useTransition();

  const handleSubmit = async (formData) => {
    startTransition(async () => {
      const result = await submitForm(formData);
      setMessage(result.message);
    });
  };

  return (
    <div>
      <SubmitFormServer action={handleSubmit} />
      {pending && <p>Submitting...</p>}
      {message && <p>{message}</p>}
    </div>
  );
}
```

**Using useTransition:**

Explain how to use the useTransition hook, to handle pending state

Explain how to improve user experience, when using useTransition.

### 3. Advanced Techniques:

**Optimistic Updates**

Explain how to perform optimistic updates, to improve the perceived performance of form submissions

Explain the benefits, and drawbacks, of optimistic updates.

### Form Validation:

Explain how to perform form validation, using react actions.

Explain how to return validation errors to the client.

Explain how to use libraries like Zod, or Yup, with react actions.

### File Uploads:

Explain how to handle file uploads using react actions.

Explain how to stream file uploads to the server.

### Authentication and Authorization:

Explain how to handle authentication, and authorization, using react actions.

### 4. Best Practices:

### Keeping Actions Focused:

We'll emphasize the importance of keeping actions focused on a single responsibility.

### Testing Actions:

Explain how to write unit tests for react actions.

### Error Handling and Logging:

Explain how to implement robust error handling and logging for actions.

By mastering React Actions, you'll be able to create streamlined and efficient form handling experiences in your React 19 applications."

## 5.2 Optimizing Data Mutations and State Updates.

"Efficient data mutations and state updates are paramount for building performant and reliable React 19 applications. In this section, we'll explore various techniques and best practices to optimize these critical operations.

### 1. Understanding Data Mutations:

### The Importance of Immutability:

We'll begin by emphasizing the importance of immutability in React state management.

Explain how mutating state directly can lead to unexpected behavior and performance issues.

Explain why react relies on referential equality to determine if a component should re-render.

### Efficient Data Structures:

We'll discuss how to use efficient data structures, such as immutable data structures or libraries like Immer, to optimize data mutations.

Explain how Immer simplifies immutable updates.

Explain the benefits of immutable data structures.

### Batching Updates:

Explain how React 19 automatically batches state updates to minimize re-renders.

Explain how to use `flushSync` when you need to force a synchronous update.

## 2. Optimizing State Updates:

### Using Functional Updates:

We'll demonstrate how to use functional updates with `useState` to avoid stale closures and ensure accurate state updates.

Example:

JavaScript

```javascript
const [count, setCount] = useState(0);

const increment = () => {
  setCount((prevCount) => prevCount + 1);
};
```

Explain why functional updates are important when the next state depends on the previous state.

### Using useReducer for Complex State:

We'll explore how `useReducer` can be used to manage complex state transitions and optimize performance.

Explain how reducers can improve state update logic.

Explain how to use `useReducer` with complex state objects.

### Memoization with useMemo and useCallback:

We'll discuss how `useMemo` and `useCallback` can be used to memoize expensive computations and prevent unnecessary re-renders during state updates.

Explain how to use these hooks to optimize performance

Explain how to use the react dev tools to analyze re-renders.

**Avoiding Unnecessary Re-renders:**

Explain how to use `React.memo` to prevent unnecessary re-renders of components

Explain how to use keys to optimize list rendering.

### 3. Optimizing Data Mutations with React Actions:

**Efficient Data Processing:**

We'll discuss how to optimize data processing within React Actions to minimize server-side load and improve response times.

Explain how to use database indexes, and efficient database queries.

Explain how to optimize api calls.

**Asynchronous Operations:**

We'll explore how to handle asynchronous operations, such as database updates or API calls, within React Actions without blocking the UI.

Explain how to handle loading states, and error states.

**Optimistic Updates:**

We will re-iterate the importance of optimistic updates, and explain how to properly implement them.

Explain how to handle rollbacks, when optimistic updates fail.

### Data Normalization:

Explain how data normalization can improve the performance of data mutations.

Explain how to use libraries like normalizr.

### 4. Best Practices:

### Profiling and Monitoring:

We'll emphasize the importance of profiling and monitoring state updates and data mutations to identify performance bottlenecks.

Explain how to use the performance tab in the browser dev tools.

### Testing State Updates and Actions:

Explain how to write unit tests for state updates and React Actions.

Explain how to test asynchronous actions.

### Documenting State Transitions and Mutations:

Explain the importance of documenting state transitions and data mutations.

By mastering these optimization techniques, you'll be able to create high-performance and reliable React 19 applications that deliver a smooth and responsive user experience."

# 5.3 Error Handling and User Feedback in Actions.

Alright, let's focus on the critical aspects of error handling and user feedback within React Actions.

"React Actions, while powerful, need robust error handling and clear user feedback to create reliable and user-friendly applications. In this section, we'll explore how to implement these essential features.

## 1. Error Handling in Actions:

### Try-Catch Blocks:

We'll demonstrate how to use `try-catch` blocks within React Actions to handle errors that may occur during server-side operations.

Explain how to catch errors from database operations, api calls, and file system operations.

Example:

JavaScript

```
// SubmitForm.server.jsx
'use server';

export async function submitForm(formData) {
  try {
    const name = formData.get('name');
    const email = formData.get('email');

    // Simulate a database operation that might fail
    if (!email.includes('@')) {
      throw new Error('Invalid email address');
    }
    // ... database or API call ...

    return { success: true, message: 'Form submitted successfully!'
};
  } catch (error) {
```

```
      console.error('Error submitting form:', error);
      return { success: false, error: error.message };
  }
}
```

## Returning Error Messages:

We'll emphasize the importance of returning informative error messages from actions to the client.

Explain how to structure error messages for clarity.

Explain how to handle different types of errors.

## Logging Errors:

Explain how to log errors on the server, for debugging purposes.

Explain how to use logging libraries

Explain how to use error monitoring tools.

## 2. User Feedback in Actions:

## Success Messages:

We'll demonstrate how to return success messages from actions to the client, providing confirmation of successful operations.

Explain how to display success messages to the user.

Example:

JavaScript

```
// SubmitForm.client.jsx
'use client';
```

```
import { useState, useTransition } from 'react';
import SubmitFormServer, { submitForm } from
'./SubmitForm.server';

export default function SubmitFormClient() {
  const [message, setMessage] = useState(null);
  const [error, setError] = useState(null);
  const [pending, startTransition] = useTransition();

  const handleSubmit = async (formData) => {
    startTransition(async () => {
      const result = await submitForm(formData);
      if (result.success) {
        setMessage(result.message);
        setError(null);
      } else {
        setError(result.error);
        setMessage(null);
      }
    });
  };

  return (
    <div>
      <SubmitFormServer action={handleSubmit} />
      {pending && <p>Submitting...</p>}
      {message && <p style={{ color: 'green' }}>{message}</p>}
      {error && <p style={{ color: 'red' }}>{error}</p>}
    </div>
  );
}
```

**Loading States:**

We'll discuss how to implement loading states to provide visual feedback during asynchronous operations.

Explain how to use the useTransition hook, to handle pending states
Explain how to display loading spinners, or progress bars.

**Validation Feedback:**

We'll explore how to provide real-time validation feedback to users, indicating errors in form input.

Explain how to return validation errors from actions.

Explain how to display validation errors next to form fields.

**Accessibility Considerations:**

Explain how to make error messages, and feedback, accessible to users with disabilities.

Explain how to use aria attributes.

**3. Advanced Techniques**

**Custom Error Components:**

Explain how to create custom error components, to display errors in a user friendly way.

**Error Boundaries**

Explain how to use error boundaries, to catch errors that occur during rendering.

**Retry Mechanisms:**

Explain how to implement retry mechanisms, for operations that fail due to network issues.

**Notifications:**

Explain how to use notification libraries, to display feedback to the user.

**4. Best Practices:**

**Clear and Concise Error Messages:**

We'll emphasize the importance of providing clear and concise error messages that are easy for users to understand.

**Consistent Feedback:**

Explain how to provide consistent feedback to the user, throughout the application.

**Testing Error Handling:**

Explain how to write unit tests for error handling in react actions.

By implementing robust error handling and clear user feedback, you'll be able to create React 19 applications that are both reliable and user-friendly."

# Chapter 6

# React 19 Routing and Navigation

## 6.1 Implementing Client-Side Routing with React Router

"React Router is the de facto standard for client-side routing in React applications. It enables us to create single-page applications (SPAs) with seamless navigation and dynamic content loading. In this section, we'll explore how to implement client-side routing using React Router.

### 1. Setting Up React Router:

### Installation:

We'll begin by demonstrating how to install React Router using npm or yarn.

Explain how to install the react-router-dom package.

Example:

Bash

npm install react-router-dom

### Wrapping Your Application:

We'll show how to wrap your application with the `BrowserRouter` component, enabling routing functionality.

Example:

JavaScript

```javascript
import { BrowserRouter } from 'react-router-dom';
import App from './App';

function Root() {
  return (
    <BrowserRouter>
      <App />
    </BrowserRouter>
  );
}

export default Root;
```

Explain the differences between BrowserRouter, HashRouter, and MemoryRouter.

## 2. Defining Routes:

**Using the `Routes` and `Route` Components:**

We'll demonstrate how to define routes using the `Routes` and `Route` components.

Explain how to define the path, and the component, that should be rendered.

Example:

JavaScript

```javascript
import { Routes, Route } from 'react-router-dom';
import Home from './Home';
```

```javascript
import About from './About';
import Contact from './Contact';

function App() {
  return (
    <Routes>
      <Route path="/" element={<Home />} />
      <Route path="/about" element={<About />} />
      <Route path="/contact" element={<Contact />} />
    </Routes>
  );
}

export default App;
```

**Nested Routes:**

We'll explore how to define nested routes, allowing for hierarchical navigation.

Explain how to use the children prop of the Route component.

Explain how to use the Outlet component to render child routes.

**Dynamic Routes:**

We'll demonstrate how to create dynamic routes with URL parameters.

Explain how to use the useParams hook to access URL parameters.

Example:

JavaScript

```
import { useParams } from 'react-router-dom';

function Product() {
  const { id } = useParams();
  return <div>Product ID: {id}</div>;
}

// ... in Routes ...
<Route path="/product/:id" element={<Product />} />
```

## 3. Navigation

**Using the `Link` Component:**

We'll show how to use the `Link` component to create navigation links within your application.

Explain how to prevent page reloads, and how to update the url.

Example:

JavaScript

```
import { Link } from 'react-router-dom';

function Navigation() {
  return (
    <nav>
      <Link to="/">Home</Link>
      <Link to="/about">About</Link>
      <Link to="/contact">Contact</Link>
    </nav>
  );
}
```

**Programmatic Navigation:**

We'll demonstrate how to perform programmatic navigation using the useNavigate hook.

Explain how to use the navigate function, to redirect the user.

Example:

JavaScript

```javascript
import { useNavigate } from 'react-router-dom';

function Login() {
  const navigate = useNavigate();

  const handleLogin = () => {
    // ... login logic ...
    navigate('/dashboard');
  };

  return <button onClick={handleLogin}>Login</button>;
}
```

**4. Advanced Techniques:**

**Route Guards:**

Explain how to create route guards, to protect routes that require authentication.

Explain how to use custom components to handle authentication logic.

### Lazy Loading Routes:

Explain how to lazy load routes, to improve performance.

Explain how to use the React.lazy and Suspense components.

### Custom Link Components:

Explain how to create custom link components, to handle active states, and other logic.

### Scroll Restoration:

Explain how to restore the scroll position, when navigating between routes.

### 5. Best Practices:

### Clear and Consistent Routing Structure:

We'll emphasize the importance of creating a clear and consistent routing structure.

### Testing Routes:

Explain how to write unit tests for routes.

### Error Handling:

Explain how to handle 404 errors, and other routing errors.

By mastering React Router, you'll be able to create robust and user-friendly client-side routing experiences in your React 19 applications."

# 6.2 Dynamic Routing and Nested Routes

"Dynamic routing and nested routes are essential for creating complex and scalable React applications. They allow us to handle dynamic content and create hierarchical navigation structures.

## 1. Dynamic Routing: Handling Variable URL Parameters

**URL Parameters with** `:paramName`:

We'll revisit how to define dynamic routes using URL parameters, denoted by `:paramName`.

Explain how to capture multiple parameters within a route.

Example:

JavaScript

```
<Route path="/products/:category/:id" element={<ProductDetail />} />
```

**Accessing Parameters with** `useParams()`:

We'll delve into how to use the `useParams()` hook to access these parameters within your components.

Explain how to handle cases where parameters are optional.

Explain how to validate parameters.

Example:

```
JavaScript
import { useParams } from 'react-router-dom';
```

```
function ProductDetail() {
  const { category, id } = useParams();
  return (
    <div>
      <h2>Product Detail</h2>
      <p>Category: {category}</p>
      <p>Product ID: {id}</p>
    </div>
  );
}
```

**Query Parameters and Search Params:**

Explain how to access query parameters, and search parameters, using the `useSearchParams` hook.

Explain how to handle url encoded parameters.

Explain how to update query parameters programmatically.

## 2. Nested Routes: Creating Hierarchical Structures

**Defining Nested Routes with `children`:**

We'll explore how to define nested routes using the `children` prop of the `Route` component.

Explain how the parent route acts as a layout for the child routes.

Example:

JavaScript

```
<Route path="/dashboard" element={<DashboardLayout />}>
  <Route index element={<DashboardHome />} />
  <Route path="profile" element={<DashboardProfile />} />
```

```
    <Route path="settings" element={<DashboardSettings />} />
  </Route>
```

**Rendering Child Routes with `<Outlet />`:**

We'll demonstrate how to use the `<Outlet />` component to render the child routes within the parent layout component.

Explain how the outlet component acts as a placeholder.

Example:

JavaScript

```
import { Outlet } from 'react-router-dom';

function DashboardLayout() {
  return (
    <div>
      <h1>Dashboard</h1>
      <nav>
        {/* Navigation links */}
      </nav>
      <main>
        <Outlet />
      </main>
    </div>
  );
}
```

**Relative Links:**

Explain how to create relative links, within nested routes.

Explain how to use the . and .. syntax.

**Index Routes:**

Explain the purpose of index routes, and how they are rendered when the parent route is matched.

Explain how to use the `index` prop of the Route component.

### 3. Advanced Techniques:

### Layout Components:

We'll discuss how to create reusable layout components for different sections of your application.

Explain how to pass props, from the parent route, to the layout component.

### Route Resolvers (Loaders):

Explain how to use loaders to fetch data before a route is rendered.

Explain how loaders improve the user experience, by preventing flashing loading states.

Explain how to handle errors inside of loaders.

### Route Actions:

Explain how to use route actions, to handle data mutations, within routes.

Explain how to use actions to handle form submissions, and other data mutations.

**Route Transitions:**

Explain how to use route transitions, to create smooth animations, when navigating between routes.

**4. Best Practices:**

**Clear and Consistent URL Structure:**

We'll emphasize the importance of creating a clear and consistent URL structure for your application.

**Separation of Concerns:**

Explain how to separate routing logic from component logic.

**Testing Dynamic and Nested Routes:**

Explain how to write unit tests for dynamic and nested routes.

**Accessibility Considerations:**

Explain how to make dynamic and nested routes accessible to users with disabilities.

By mastering dynamic routing and nested routes, you'll be able to create complex and scalable React 19 applications with seamless navigation and dynamic content loading."

# 6.3 Server side routing considerations.

"While React Router excels at client-side routing, the introduction of server components in React 19 necessitates a deeper understanding of server-side routing considerations. This section explores how to effectively bridge the gap between client and server routing.

# 1. Understanding the Dual Nature of Routing:

## Client-Side vs. Server-Side Routing:

We'll begin by clarifying the distinction between client-side routing (handled by React Router) and server-side routing (handled by your server).

Explain how client-side routing happens after the initial page load, and server-side routing happens before.

Explain how server components change the dynamic of client vs server side routing.

## The Role of Server Components:

We'll discuss how server components influence routing by enabling server-side rendering of specific parts of your application.

Explain how server components can be used to render different content, based on the URL.

# 2. Server-Side Rendering and Initial Page Loads:

## Handling Initial Requests:

We'll explore how your server handles initial requests and renders the appropriate HTML for the requested URL.

Explain how to configure your server to handle different routes.

Explain how to use server side rendering with node.js, or other server side technologies.

## Data Fetching on the Server:

We'll emphasize the importance of fetching data on the server for initial page loads, especially for SEO and performance.

Explain how to fetch data inside of server components.

Explain how to pass data from server components, to client components.

## Code Splitting and Lazy Loading:

Explain how to code split, and lazy load, components on the server.

Explain how to use dynamic imports on the server.

## 3. Integration with React Router:

### Server-Side Rendering with React Router:

We'll discuss how to integrate React Router with server-side rendering, ensuring that the initial HTML matches the client-side routing logic.

Explain how to use server side rendering with react router.

Explain how to handle redirects, and 404 errors, on the server.

### Handling Client-Side Navigation:

We'll clarify how React Router takes over routing after the initial page load, handling subsequent navigation on the client.

Explain how client side routing interacts with server side routing.

### Server-Side Data Prefetching:

Explain how to prefetch data on the server, before the client side route is rendered.

Explain how to use route loaders, to prefetch data.

## 4. Advanced Server-Side Routing Considerations:

### Authentication and Authorization:

We'll explore how to handle authentication and authorization on the server, protecting sensitive routes and data

Explain how to use server side middleware, to handle authentication.

Explain how to use cookies, and sessions, to manage user authentication.

### SEO Optimization:

We'll discuss how server-side rendering and proper URL structure contribute to SEO optimization.

Explain how to use server side rendering to generate meta tags.

Explain how to use sitemaps, and robots.txt.

### Caching Strategies:

We'll delve into various caching strategies for server-side routing, including:

CDN caching

Server-side caching

HTTP caching

Explain how to use caching headers.

### API Routing:

Explain how to create api routes, on the server.

Explain how to handle api requests, and responses.

## 5. Best Practices:

### Consistency Between Client and Server:

We'll emphasize the importance of maintaining consistency between client-side and server-side routing logic.

### Performance Optimization:

Explain how to optimize server side rendering performance.

### Error Handling:

Explain how to handle server side routing errors.

### Security Considerations:

Explain how to secure server side routes.

By understanding these server-side routing considerations, you'll be able to build robust and performant React 19 applications that seamlessly bridge the gap between client and server."

# Chapter 7

# State Management in React 19: Beyond useState

## 7.1 Exploring Context API and Reducers for Complex State

"As React applications grow in complexity, managing state effectively becomes crucial. The Context API and reducers provide robust solutions for handling complex state, especially when dealing with data that needs to be shared across multiple components.[1]

### 1. Context API: Sharing Data Across the Component Tree

**Creating Contexts with `createContext()`:**

We'll revisit how to create contexts using `createContext()`, emphasizing its role in providing a way to share values between components without explicitly passing props through every level of the tree.

Explain how to create a default value for the context.

Example:

JavaScript

import { createContext } from 'react';

const UserContext = createContext(null);

**Providing Context Values with `<Provider>`:**

We'll demonstrate how to use the `<Provider>` component to wrap a section of the component tree and provide a context value.

Explain how to update the context value.

Example:

JavaScript

```javascript
import { useState } from 'react';

function UserProvider({ children }) {
  const [user, setUser] = useState({ name: 'Guest' });

  return (
    <UserContext.Provider value={{ user, setUser }}>
    {children}
    </UserContext.Provider>
  );
}
```

**Consuming Context Values with `useContext()`:**

We'll explore how to use the `useContext()` hook to access context values within functional components.

Explain how to handle cases where the context value is undefined.

Example:

JavaScript
```javascript
import { useContext } from 'react';
```

```javascript
function UserProfile() {
  const { user } = useContext(UserContext);

  return <p>Welcome, {user.name}!</p>;
}
```

**Context Performance Considerations:**

We'll discuss how context updates trigger re-renders in consuming components and how to optimize performance.

Explain how to use memoization with context values.

Explain how to use separate contexts for different parts of the state.

## 2. Reducers: Managing Complex State Logic

**Defining Reducers with useReducer():**

We'll delve into how to define reducers using useReducer(), emphasizing their role in managing complex state transitions.

Explain how to define the initial state, and the reducer function.

Example:

JavaScript

```javascript
import { useReducer } from 'react';

const initialState = { count: 0 };

function reducer(state, action) {
  switch (action.type) {
    case 'increment':
      return { count: state.count + 1 };
```

```
    case 'decrement':
      return { count: state.count - 1 };
    default:
      throw new Error();
  }
}

function Counter() {
  const [state, dispatch] = useReducer(reducer, initialState);

  return (
    <div>
      <p>Count: {state.count}</p>
          <button onClick={() => dispatch({ type: 'increment'
})}>Increment</button>
          <button onClick={() => dispatch({ type: 'decrement'
})}>Decrement</button>
    </div>
  );
}
```

**Dispatching[2] Actions:**

We'll demonstrate how to dispatch actions to trigger state updates using the dispatch function returned by useReducer().

Explain how to pass data with actions.

**Handling Complex State Transitions:**

We'll explore how reducers can handle complex state transitions, such as updating nested objects or arrays, in a predictable and efficient manner.

Explain how to handle asynchronous actions with reducers.

**Benefits of using useReducer:**

Explain how useReducer can improve testability.

Explain how useReducer can improve predictability.

## 3. Combining Context API and Reducers:

**Centralized State Management:**

We'll discuss how to combine Context API and reducers to create a centralized state management solution for your application.

Explain how to use the reducer to update the context value.

Example:

JavaScript

```javascript
import { createContext, useReducer, useContext } from 'react';

const AppContext = createContext();

const initialState = { count: 0 };

function reducer(state, action) {
  // ... reducer logic ...
}

function AppProvider({ children }) {
  const [state, dispatch] = useReducer(reducer, initialState);

  return (
    <AppContext.Provider value={{ state, dispatch }}>
      {children}
    </AppContext.Provider>
  );
```

```
}

function CounterDisplay() {
  const { state } = useContext(AppContext);
  return <p>Count: {state.count}</p>;
}

function CounterButtons() {
  const { dispatch } = useContext(AppContext);
  return (
    <div>
          <button onClick={() => dispatch({ type: 'increment'
})}>Increment</button>
          <button onClick={() => dispatch({ type: 'decrement'
})}>Decrement</button>
    </div>
  );
}
```

**Benefits of Combined Approach:**

We'll highlight the benefits of using this combined approach, such as improved code organization, maintainability, and testability.

Explain how this approach simplifies state updates.

**4. Best Practices:**

**Keeping Reducers Pure:**

We'll emphasize the importance of keeping reducers pure functions, meaning they should not have side effects and should always return a new state object.

**Action Types as Constants:**

Explain the importance of using action types as constants.

**Testing Reducers and Contexts:**

Explain how to write unit tests for reducers and contexts.

By mastering the combination of Context API and reducers, you'll be able to effectively manage complex state in your React 19 applications, creating scalable and maintainable solutions."

# 7.2 Integrating External State Management Libraries (e.g., Zustand, Recoil)

"While React's built-in state management tools like useState, useReducer, and Context API are powerful, external state management libraries like Zustand and Recoil offer additional features and benefits for complex applications. In this section, we'll explore how to integrate these libraries into your React 19 projects.

## 1. Understanding External State Management Libraries:

**Zustand: Simple and Scalable State Management:**

We'll introduce Zustand, emphasizing its simplicity and ease of use.

Explain how Zustand uses a simple store with setters and getters.

Explain how Zustand minimizes re-renders

## Recoil: Fine-Grained State Management:

We'll introduce Recoil, highlighting its fine-grained state management capabilities and efficient data flow.

Explain how Recoil uses atoms and selectors.

Explain how Recoil handles derived state.

## When to Use External Libraries:

We'll discuss the scenarios where external state management libraries are most beneficial, such as:

Large and complex applications with shared state.

Applications with complex data dependencies.

Applications requiring fine-grained control over state updates.

## 2. Integrating Zustand:

## Installation and Setup:

We'll demonstrate how to install Zustand using npm or yarn.

Explain how to create a Zustand store.

Example:

Bash

```
npm install zustand
```

JavaScript

```
import create from 'zustand';

const useStore = create((set) => ({
```

```
  count: 0,
  increment: () => set((state) => ({ count: state.count + 1 })),
  decrement: () => set((state) => ({ count: state.count - 1 })),
}));
```

**Using the Store in Components:**

We'll show how to use the Zustand store within your React components.

Explain how to select specific parts of the store.

Example:

JavaScript

```
import useStore from './store';

function Counter() {
  const count = useStore((state) => state.count);
  const increment = useStore((state) => state.increment);
  const decrement = useStore((state) => state.decrement);

  return (
   <div>
     <p>Count: {count}</p>
     <button onClick={increment}>Increment</button>
     <button onClick={decrement}>Decrement</button>
   </div>
  );
}
```

**Zustand Middleware:**

Explain how to use Zustand middleware, for things like logging, or persisting state.

## 3. Integrating Recoil:

**Installation and Setup:**

We'll demonstrate how to install Recoil using npm or yarn.

Explain how to wrap the application with the RecoilRoot component.

Example:

Bash

```
npm install recoil
```

JavaScript

```
import { RecoilRoot } from 'recoil';
import App from './App';

function Root() {
  return (
    <RecoilRoot>
     <App />
    </RecoilRoot>
  );
}

export default Root;
```

## Defining Atoms and Selectors:

We'll explore how to define atoms for basic state and selectors for derived state.

Explain how to use the useRecoilState, and useRecoilValue hooks.

Example:

JavaScript

```
import { atom, selector, useRecoilState, useRecoilValue } from 'recoil';

const countState = atom({
  key: 'countState',
  default: 0,
});

const doubleCountState = selector({
  key: 'doubleCountState',
  get: ({ get }) => get(countState) * 2,
});

function Counter() {
  const [count, setCount] = useRecoilState(countState);
  const doubleCount = useRecoilValue(doubleCountState);

  return (
    <div>
      <p>Count: {count}</p>
      <p>Double Count: {doubleCount}</p>
              <button   onClick={()   =>   setCount(count   +
1)}>Increment</button>
```

```
    </div>
  );
}
```

## Recoil's Asynchronous Data Flow:

Explain how Recoil handles asynchronous data fetching, and derived data.

## 4. Best Practices:

### Choosing the Right Library:

We'll discuss how to choose the right state management library based on your application's needs.

### Avoiding Overuse:

We'll caution against overusing external state management libraries for simple applications.

### Testing External State:

Explain how to write unit tests for code that uses external state management libraries.

### Performance Monitoring:

Explain how to monitor the performance of external state management libraries.

By understanding how to integrate external state management libraries like Zustand and Recoil, you'll be able to effectively manage complex state in your React 19 applications, creating scalable and maintainable solutions."

# 7.3 State Management best practices.

"Effective state management is crucial for building scalable and maintainable React 19 applications. This section outlines best practices to guide you in making informed decisions about state management.

**1. Principles of Effective State Management:**

**Single Source of Truth:**

Emphasize the importance of having a single source of truth for your application's state.

Explain how this prevents inconsistencies and simplifies debugging.

**Immutability:**

Reinforce the significance of immutability in state updates

Explain how immutability ensures predictable state transitions and optimizes performance.

Explain how to use the spread operator, and object.assign, to create copies of state.

**Predictable State Transitions:**

Stress the need for predictable state transitions, making it easier to understand and debug your application.

Explain how reducers can help with predictable state transitions.

**Separation of Concerns:**

Advocate for separating state management logic from component logic

Explain how custom hooks, and external state management libraries, can help with this.

## 2. Choosing the Right State Management Approach:

### Local State (`useState`):

Discuss when to use local state for component-specific data.

Explain the limitations of local state for sharing data between components.

### Context API:

Explain when to use Context API for sharing data across the component tree.

Discuss the performance considerations of Context API.

Explain how to avoid unnecessary re-renders with context.

### Reducers (`useReducer`):

Discuss when to use reducers for managing complex state transitions.

Explain the benefits of reducers for predictability and testability.

### External State Management Libraries (Zustand, Recoil):

Discuss when to use external libraries for large and complex applications.

Explain the trade-offs between built-in and external state management solutions.

Explain how to choose the right library for your needs.

### 3. Best Practices for State Updates:

**Functional Updates:**

Emphasize the use of functional updates with `useState` to avoid stale closures.

Explain why functional updates are essential for asynchronous state updates.

**Batching Updates:**

Explain how React automatically batches state updates to optimize performance.

Explain when to use flushSync.

**Memoization:**

Discuss how to use `useMemo` and `useCallback` to memoize expensive computations and prevent unnecessary re-renders.

Explain how to use the react dev tools, to analyze re-renders.

**Avoiding Unnecessary State:**

Advocate for keeping state minimal and avoiding unnecessary state variables.

Explain how derived state, can reduce the amount of state that is needed.

### 4. Best Practices for State Organization:

**Colocating State:**

Discuss when to colocate state with the components that use it.

Explain how colocation improves code organization.

### Lifting State Up:

Explain when to lift state up to a common ancestor component when multiple components need access to the same data.

### Normalizing State:

Explain the benefits of normalizing state, especially when dealing with complex data structures.

Explain how to use libraries like normalizr.

### Using Selectors:

Explain the benefits of using selectors, to derive state.

Explain how selectors can improve performance.

### 5. Testing and Debugging:

### Unit Testing State Logic:

Emphasize the importance of unit testing state management logic, including reducers and custom hooks.

Explain how to test asynchronous state updates.

### Debugging Tools:

Discuss how to use React DevTools and other debugging tools to inspect and debug state.

Explain how to use browser dev tools, to analyze performance.

### Logging State Changes:

Explain how to log state changes, for debugging purposes.

## 6. Performance Considerations:

### Profiling and Monitoring:

Advocate for profiling and monitoring state updates to identify performance bottlenecks.

Explain how to use the performance tab in the browser dev tools.

### Avoiding Deep Object Comparisons:

Explain how deep object comparisons can impact performance.

Explain how to use shallow comparisons.

### Code Splitting:

Explain how code splitting can improve the initial load time of your application.

By adhering to these state management best practices, you'll be able to build robust, scalable, and maintainable React 19 applications that deliver a smooth and efficient user experience."

# Chapter 8

# Performance Optimization in React 19

## 8.1 Identifying and Resolving Performance Bottlenecks

"Performance is a critical aspect of any web application. Identifying and resolving performance bottlenecks in your React 19 applications is essential for delivering a smooth and responsive user experience. In this section, we'll explore techniques and tools to help you optimize your application's performance.

### 1. Identifying Performance Bottlenecks:

### Profiling with Browser Developer Tools:

We'll begin by discussing how to use the Performance tab in browser developer tools to profile your application's performance.

Explain how to record performance profiles, and how to analyze the results.

Explain how to identify long running tasks, and expensive function calls.

### React Developer Tools:

We'll explore how to use the React Developer Tools to identify performance issues related to component rendering.

Explain how to use the profiler tab, to identify components that are re-rendering unnecessarily.

Explain how to analyze the component tree, for performance issues.

**Performance Monitoring Tools:**

Explain how to use performance monitoring tools, to track performance metrics in production.

Explain how to use tools like Lighthouse, to analyze website performance.

**User Experience Metrics:**

Explain how to track user experience metrics, such as First Contentful Paint (FCP), Largest Contentful Paint (LCP), and Cumulative Layout Shift (CLS).

Explain how to use these metrics, to identify performance issues.

**2. Common Performance Bottlenecks:**

**Unnecessary Re-renders:**

We'll discuss how unnecessary re-renders can impact performance, especially in large component trees.

Explain how to use `React.memo`, `useMemo`, and `useCallback` to prevent unnecessary re-renders.

Explain how to use the react dev tools, to identify re-renders.

**Expensive Computations:**

We'll explore how expensive computations can slow down your application.

Explain how to use web workers, to offload expensive computations.

Explain how to use memoization, to cache expensive computations.

**Large Bundle Sizes:**

We'll discuss how large bundle sizes can increase initial load times.

Explain how to use code splitting, and lazy loading, to reduce bundle sizes.

Explain how to use tree shaking, to remove unused code.

**Network Requests:**

We'll explore how network requests can impact performance, especially when fetching large amounts of data.

Explain how to use caching, to reduce network requests.

Explain how to optimize api calls.

**DOM Manipulations:**

Explain how excessive DOM manipulations can impact performance.

Explain how react optimizes DOM manipulations.

Explain how to avoid directly manipulating the DOM.

**3. Resolving Performance Bottlenecks:**

**Optimizing Component Rendering:**

We'll demonstrate how to optimize component rendering using `React.memo`, `useMemo`, and `useCallback`.

Explain how to use shouldComponentUpdate, in class components.

**Memoizing Expensive Computations:**

We'll show how to memoize expensive computations using `useMemo`.

**Code Splitting and Lazy Loading:**

We'll demonstrate how to implement code splitting and lazy loading using `React.lazy` and `Suspense`.

**Optimizing Network Requests:**

We'll discuss how to optimize network requests by using caching, compression, and efficient data fetching techniques.

**Using Web Workers:**

Explain how to use web workers, to offload expensive computations.

**Image Optimization:**

Explain how to optimize images, for web performance

Explain how to use image compression, and lazy loading.

**Font Optimization:**

Explain how to optimize font loading, for web performance.

### 4. Best Practices:

### Performance Budgeting:

We'll emphasize the importance of setting performance budgets and monitoring performance metrics.

Explain how to set performance budgets, and how to track them.

### Continuous Performance Monitoring:

Explain the importance of continuous performance monitoring, in production.

### Testing Performance Improvements:

Explain how to test performance improvements, before deploying them.

By mastering the techniques for identifying and resolving performance bottlenecks, you'll be able to create high-performance React 19 applications that deliver a smooth and responsive user experience."

# 8.2 Code Splitting, Lazy Loading, and Memoization Techniques

"To ensure optimal performance in React 19 applications, we must leverage code splitting, lazy loading, and memoization. These techniques help reduce initial load times, minimize unnecessary computations, and improve overall responsiveness.

# 1. Code Splitting: Reducing Initial Bundle Size

## The Concept of Code Splitting:

We'll begin by explaining the concept of code splitting, which involves dividing your application's code into smaller chunks that can be loaded on demand.

Explain how this reduces the initial bundle size, and improves initial load times.

## Route-Based Code Splitting:

We'll demonstrate how to implement route-based code splitting using React Router and `React.lazy`.

Example:

JavaScript

```javascript
import React, { lazy, Suspense } from 'react';
import { BrowserRouter as Router, Routes, Route } from 'react-router-dom';

const Home = lazy(() => import('./components/Home'));
const About = lazy(() => import('./components/About'));
const Contact = lazy(() => import('./components/Contact'));

function App() {
  return (
    <Router>
      <Suspense fallback={<div>Loading...</div>}>
        <Routes>
          <Route path="/" element={<Home />} />
          <Route path="/about" element={<About />} />
          <Route path="/contact" element={<Contact />} />
        </Routes>
```

```
    </Suspense>
  </Router>
 );
}
```

export default App;

Explain how the Suspense component handles loading states.

**Component-Based Code Splitting:**

We'll explore how to implement component-based code splitting using `React.lazy` for components that are only rendered under specific conditions.

Explain how to split components that are used in modals, or other conditional rendering scenarios.

**Dynamic Imports:**

Explain how dynamic imports work, and how they are used for code splitting.

Explain how to use dynamic imports outside of react components.

**Webpack and Vite Configuration:**

Explain how to configure webpack, or vite, for code splitting.

Explain how to use chunk names, to control the naming of code split chunks.

## 2. Lazy Loading: Loading Resources on Demand

**The Concept of Lazy Loading:**

We'll discuss the concept of lazy loading, which involves deferring the loading of resources until they are needed.

Explain how lazy loading improves performance, by reducing the amount of resources that are loaded initially.

**Lazy Loading Images and Videos:**

We'll demonstrate how to lazy load images and videos using the `loading="lazy"` attribute.

Explain how to use the Intersection Observer API, for more advanced lazy loading techniques.

Example:

JavaScript

```
<img src="large-image.jpg" loading="lazy" alt="Large Image" />
```

**Lazy Loading Components:**

We will re-iterate how to lazy load components, using React.lazy.

**Lazy Loading Data:**

Explain how to lazy load data, using techniques like infinite scrolling, or pagination.

Explain how to use the Intersection Observer API, to trigger data loading.

### 3. Memoization: Caching Expensive Computations

**The Concept of Memoization:**

We'll revisit the concept of memoization, which involves caching the results of expensive function calls and returning the cached result when the same inputs occur again.[1]

Explain how memoization prevents redundant computations.

**Memoizing Component Rendering with `React.memo`:**

We'll demonstrate how to use `React.memo` to memoize component rendering, preventing unnecessary re-renders when props haven't changed.

Example:

JavaScript

```javascript
import React from 'react';

const MyComponent = React.memo(({ data }) => {
  // Component rendering logic
  return <div>{data}</div>;
});
```

Explain how to use a custom comparison function, with React.memo.

**Memoizing Computed Values with `useMemo`:**

We'll revisit how to use `useMemo` to memoize the results of expensive computations.

Explain how the dependency array controls when the memoized value is recalculated.

**Memoizing Callback Functions with** `useCallback`**:**

We'll revisit how to use `useCallback` to memoize callback functions, preventing unnecessary re-renders in child components.

Explain how to use useCallback with useEffect.

**4. Best Practices:**

**Profiling and Measuring Performance:**

We'll emphasize the importance of profiling and measuring performance before and after implementing these techniques.

**Avoiding Over-Optimization:**

We'll caution against over-optimizing, as it can lead to unnecessary complexity.

**Testing Performance Improvements:**

Explain how to test performance improvements, before deploying them.

By mastering code splitting, lazy loading, and memoization, you'll be able to significantly enhance the performance of your React 19 applications, creating smooth and responsive user experiences."

# 8.3 React 19's performance enhancing features.

"React 19 comes packed with features designed to boost performance and streamline your development workflow. Let's explore these enhancements and understand how they contribute to creating faster and more efficient applications.

# 1. Server Components: A Performance Powerhouse

## Reduced Client-Side JavaScript:

We'll reiterate how server components minimize the amount of JavaScript sent to the client, leading to faster initial page loads and improved performance on low-powered devices.

Explain how this reduces the time to interactive (TTI).

## Data Fetching on the Server:

We'll emphasize how server components enable data fetching directly on the server, reducing network latency and improving data security.

Explain how this reduces the number of round trips to the server.

## Streaming Rendering Improvements:

Explain how react 19 improves upon the streaming rendering architecture, making it even faster.

# 2. React Actions: Optimizing Data Mutations

## Reduced Client-Server Round Trips:

We'll discuss how React Actions streamline data mutations, minimizing the number of client-server round trips and improving overall performance.

Explain how this reduces network latency.

## Optimistic Updates:

We will re-iterate how optimistic updates, when used correctly, can greatly improve the perceived performance of an application.

## 3. React Compiler

**Automatic Memoization:**

Explain how the react compiler will automatically memoize components, and values, reducing the amount of manual memoization that is needed.

Explain how this will improve performance, by reducing unnecessary re-renders.

**Improved Performance:**

Explain how the react compiler will optimize react code, resulting in better performance.

Explain how the react compiler will analyze the react code, to find performance bottlenecks.

## 4. Enhanced Hooks and APIs:

**Optimized `useMemo` and `useCallback`:**

We'll discuss how React 19 optimizes `useMemo` and `useCallback`, reducing the overhead of memoization and improving performance.

Explain how these hooks are now more efficient.

**Automatic Batching:**

Explain how react 19 improves automatic batching of state updates, resulting in fewer re-renders.

Explain how this improves performance, by reducing the amount of work that react has to do.

### Transitions:

Explain how the useTransition hook, allows for non blocking UI updates.

Explain how transitions improve the user experience, by keeping the UI responsive.

## 5. Performance Improvements Under the Hood:

### Improved Reconciliation Algorithm:

Explain how the react core team is always working on improving the reconciliation algorithm, resulting in better performance.

### Optimized Rendering Pipeline:

Explain how the react core team is always working on optimizing the rendering pipeline, resulting in faster rendering.

## 6. Best Practices to Maximize Performance:

### Use Production Builds:

We'll emphasize the importance of using production builds for optimal performance.

Explain how production builds are optimized for performance.

### Profile and Measure Performance:

We'll reiterate the importance of profiling and measuring performance to identify and address bottlenecks.

### Keep Components Small and Focused:

Explain how small and focused components, improve performance.

**Avoid Deep Component Trees:**

Explain how deep component trees, can impact performance.

**Use Keys Effectively:**

Explain how to use keys effectively, when rendering lists.

By understanding and leveraging these performance-enhancing features, you'll be able to create React 19 applications that are not only feature-rich but also incredibly fast and responsive."

# Chapter 9

# Building Practical Projects: E-commerce Store with React 19

## 9.1 Developing a Product Listing and Shopping Cart

"Building a product listing and shopping cart is a fundamental step in creating an e-commerce application. In this section, we'll walk through the process of developing these features using React 19, focusing on best practices and efficient state management.

### 1. Setting Up the Project Structure:

**Component Organization:**

We'll begin by establishing a clear and organized component structure for our e-commerce application.

Explain how to create components for product listings, product details, and the shopping cart.

Example:

```
src/
  components/
    ProductList/
      ProductList.jsx
      ProductList.css
    ProductCard/
      ProductCard.jsx
      ProductCard.css
    ProductDetails/
```

```
    ProductDetails.jsx
    ProductDetails.css
  ShoppingCart/
    ShoppingCart.jsx
    ShoppingCart.css
  CartItem/
    CartItem.jsx
    CartItem.css
```

## Data Structure:

We'll define the data structure for our products, including properties like name, price, image, and description.

Explain how to create a mock product data array, or how to fetch product data from an API.

## 2. Building the Product Listing:

### Fetching Product Data:

We'll demonstrate how to fetch product data from an API or use a mock data array.

Explain how to use useEffect, to fetch data.

If using server components, explain how to fetch data directly on the server.

### Rendering Product Cards:

We'll create a `ProductCard` component to display individual product information.

Explain how to use props, to pass product data to the ProductCard component.

Explain how to use CSS modules, or styled components, for styling.

**Displaying Product List:**

We'll create a `ProductList` component to render the product cards in a grid or list layout.

Explain how to use map, to iterate over the product data.

Explain how to handle loading states, and error states.

**3. Implementing the Shopping Cart:**

**State Management:**

We'll discuss how to manage the shopping cart state using `useState` or `useReducer`.

Explain how to use context api, or an external state management library, for more complex applications.

**Adding Items to the Cart:**

We'll implement a function to add items to the shopping cart when a user clicks the "Add to Cart" button.

Explain how to update the cart state immutably.

**Displaying Cart Items:**

We'll create a `CartItem` component to display individual items in the shopping cart.

Explain how to display the item name, quantity, and price.

## Calculating Cart Total:

We'll implement a function to calculate the total price of items in the shopping cart.

Explain how to use reduce, to calculate the total price.

## Updating Cart Quantities

We'll implement functionality to allow users to update the quantity of items in the cart.

Explain how to handle incrementing, and decrementing, item quantities.

## Removing Items from the Cart:

We'll implement a function to remove items from the shopping cart.

Explain how to filter the cart items, to remove an item.

## Displaying Cart Summary:

We'll create a `ShoppingCart` component to display the cart items and the total price.

Explain how to display the cart summary in a modal, or a sidebar.

## 4. Enhancing User Experience:

## Adding Product Details Page:

We'll create a `ProductDetails` component to display detailed information about a selected product.

Explain how to use react router, to navigate to the product details page.

Explain how to fetch product details, based on the product id.

**Implementing Search and Filtering:**

We'll implement search and filtering functionality to allow users to find products easily.

Explain how to use the filter, and search, methods on arrays.

**Adding Loading Indicators:**

We'll add loading indicators to provide feedback to users during data fetching.

**Improving Accessibility:**

We'll ensure that the application is accessible to users with disabilities by using ARIA attributes and semantic HTML.

**5. Best Practices:**

**Component Reusability:**

Emphasize the importance of creating reusable components.

**State Management:**

Explain how to choose the right state management approach.

**Performance Optimization:**

Explain how to optimize the performance of the application.

**Testing:**

Explain how to write unit tests for the components.

By following these steps, you'll be able to create a functional and user-friendly product listing and shopping cart in your React 19 e-commerce application."

## 9.2 Implementing User Authentication and Order Management

"User authentication and order management are essential components of a robust e-commerce application. In this section, we'll explore how to implement these features using React 19, focusing on security and user experience.

**1. User Authentication:**

**Authentication Flow:**

We'll outline the authentication flow, including registration, login, and logout.

Explain how to use a backend service, like Firebase Authentication, Auth0, or a custom backend, for user authentication.

**Registration:**

We'll create a registration form for new users to create accounts.

Explain how to handle form submissions, and how to send user data to the backend.

Explain how to hash passwords, before storing them in the database.

**Login:**

We'll create a login form for existing users to authenticate.

Explain how to handle form submissions, and how to verify user credentials with the backend.

Explain how to store authentication tokens, in local storage, or cookies.

**Logout:**

We'll implement a logout function to clear user authentication tokens and redirect users to the login page.

Explain how to clear authentication tokens.

**Protected Routes:**

We'll create protected routes that require authentication to access.

Explain how to use React Router to implement route guards.

Example:

JavaScript

```javascript
import { Navigate, Outlet } from 'react-router-dom';
import { useAuth } from './AuthContext';

function ProtectedRoute() {
  const { isAuthenticated } = useAuth();
  return isAuthenticated ? <Outlet /> : <Navigate to="/login" />;
}
```

**Authentication Context:**

We'll create an authentication context to manage user authentication state and provide authentication functions to components.

Explain how to use the context api, to manage authentication state.

Explain how to use custom hooks, to access the authentication context.

## 2. Order Management:

### Order Data Structure:

We'll define the data structure for orders, including properties like order ID, user ID, items, total price, and shipping address.

Explain how to store order data in a database.

### Placing Orders:

We'll implement a function to place orders, including validating order data and sending it to the backend.

Explain how to use react actions, to submit order data to the server.

Explain how to handle payment processing.

### Order History:

We'll create an order history page to display users' past orders.

Explain how to fetch order data from the backend.

Explain how to display order details.

### Order Details:

We'll create an order details page to display detailed information about a specific order.

Explain how to use react router, to navigate to the order details page.

Explain how to fetch order details, based on the order id.

## Order Status Tracking:

We'll implement functionality to track the status of orders, such as "Pending," "Shipped," and "Delivered."

Explain how to update order status, on the backend.

Explain how to display order status updates, to the user.

### 3. Enhancing User Experience:

### User Profile Page:

We'll create a user profile page to allow users to view and update their personal information.

Explain how to fetch user data from the backend.

Explain how to handle form submissions, to update user data.

### Address Management:

We'll implement functionality to allow users to manage their shipping addresses.

Explain how to store user addresses, in the database.

### Payment Integration:

Explain how to integrate with payment gateways, like Stripe, or PayPal.

Explain how to use react libraries for payment integration.

### Email Notifications:

Explain how to send email notifications, for order confirmations, and shipping updates.

### Security Considerations:

Explain how to protect user data, and how to prevent common security vulnerabilities.

Explain how to use HTTPS, and how to prevent cross site scripting (XSS) attacks.

### 4. Best Practices:

### Security:

Emphasize the importance of security in user authentication and order management.

### User Experience:

Explain how to create a seamless and user-friendly experience.

### Testing:

Explain how to write unit tests for authentication and order management logic.

### Error Handling:

Explain how to handle errors gracefully, and how to provide informative error messages.

By implementing user authentication and order management, you'll be able to create a complete and functional e-commerce application with React 19."

# 9.3 Integrating Payment Gateways and APIs.

"Integrating payment gateways and APIs is essential for enabling secure and seamless online transactions in your e-commerce application. In this section, we'll explore how to integrate popular payment gateways and APIs with React 19.

## 1. Understanding Payment Gateways and APIs:

### Payment Gateway Overview:

We'll provide an overview of popular payment gateways like Stripe, PayPal, and Square, highlighting their features and benefits.

Explain the differences between payment gateways, and payment processors.

### API Integration:

We'll discuss how to integrate payment gateway APIs with React 19, focusing on security and best practices.

Explain how to use server side api calls, to handle payment processing.

## 2. Integrating Stripe:

### Setting Up a Stripe Account:

We'll guide you through the process of setting up a Stripe account and obtaining API keys.

### Stripe Elements:

We'll demonstrate how to use Stripe Elements to create secure and customizable payment forms.

Example:

JavaScript

```
import { Elements, CardElement, useStripe, useElements } from
'@stripe/react-stripe-js';
import { loadStripe } from '@stripe/stripe-js';

const                     stripePromise                     =
loadStripe('YOUR_STRIPE_PUBLISHABLE_KEY');

function CheckoutForm() {
  const stripe = useStripe();
  const elements = useElements();

  const handleSubmit = async (event) => {
    event.preventDefault();

    if (!stripe || !elements) {
      return;
    }

    const cardElement = elements.getElement(CardElement);

            const  {  error,  paymentMethod  }  =  await
stripe.createPaymentMethod({
      type: 'card',
      card: cardElement,
    });

    if (error) {
      console.log('[stripe error]', error);
    } else {
      console.log('[PaymentMethod]', paymentMethod);
      // Send paymentMethod.id to your server
    }
  };

  return (
```

```
  <form onSubmit={handleSubmit}>
    <CardElement />
    <button type="submit" disabled={!stripe}>
      Pay
    </button>
  </form>
  );
}

function StripeCheckout() {
  return (
    <Elements stripe={stripePromise}>
      <CheckoutForm />
    </Elements>
  );
}
```

**Server-Side Integration:**

We'll discuss how to integrate Stripe with your server-side application to process payments securely.

Explain how to create server side api calls, to create payment intents.

Explain how to handle webhooks, to receive payment confirmation.

**Handling Payment Errors:**

Explain how to handle payment errors, and how to display error messages to the user.

### 3. Integrating PayPal:

### Setting Up a PayPal Developer Account:

We'll guide you through the process of setting up a PayPal developer account and obtaining API credentials.

### PayPal JavaScript SDK:

We'll demonstrate how to use the PayPal JavaScript SDK to integrate PayPal payments into your React 19 application.

Explain how to use the PayPal buttons.

### Server-Side Integration:

We'll discuss how to integrate PayPal with your server-side application to process payments securely.

Explain how to create server side api calls, to create orders.

Explain how to handle webhooks, to receive payment confirmation.

### Handling Payment Errors:

Explain how to handle payment errors, and how to display error messages to the user.

### 4. Integrating Other Payment APIs:

### Custom Payment Integrations:

We'll discuss how to integrate other payment APIs, such as Square and others, using similar principles.

Explain how to read the api documentation, and how to use the api.

## API Documentation:

Emphasize the importance of reading and understanding the API documentation for each payment gateway.

## 5. Security Considerations:

### PCI Compliance:

We'll discuss the importance of PCI compliance and how to ensure your application meets security standards.

Explain how payment gateways handle PCI compliance.

### Tokenization:

Explain how tokenization protects sensitive payment information.

### HTTPS:

Reiterate the importance of using HTTPS to secure data transmission.

### Server-Side Security:

Explain how to secure server side api calls, that handle payment processing.

Explain how to protect api keys.

## 6. Best Practices:

### Testing Payment Integrations:

We'll emphasize the importance of thoroughly testing payment integrations in a sandbox environment.

Explain how to use test cards, and test accounts.

**Error Handling:**

Explain how to implement robust error handling for payment processing.

**User Experience:**

Explain how to create a seamless and user-friendly checkout experience.

**Documentation:**

Explain the importance of documenting payment integrations.

By integrating payment gateways and APIs, you'll be able to create a secure and functional e-commerce application that enables seamless online transactions."

# Chapter 10

# Advanced React 19: Testing, Deployment, and Best Practices

## 10.1 Writing Effective Unit and Integration Tests with Jest and React Testing Library

"Testing is an indispensable part of software development, especially in React 19 applications. Jest and React Testing Library provide a powerful combination for writing unit and integration tests, ensuring code quality and reliability.

### 1. Setting Up Jest and React Testing Library:

### Installation:

We'll demonstrate how to install Jest and React Testing Library using npm or yarn.

Example:

Bash

```
npm install --save-dev jest @testing-library/react @testing-library/jest-dom
```

### Configuration:

We'll discuss how to configure Jest and React Testing Library for your project, including setting up test scripts and configuration files.

Explain how to create a jest.config.js file.

Explain how to add test scripts to the package.json file.

**Setting up Test Environment:**

Explain how to set up a test environment, that mimics the browser environment.

**2. Writing Unit Tests with Jest:**

**Testing Individual Components:**

We'll demonstrate how to write unit tests for individual components using Jest.

Explain how to use the `describe` and `it` blocks, to organize tests.

Explain how to use the `expect` function, to make assertions.

Example:

JavaScript

```
// Button.test.jsx
import React from 'react';
import { render, screen } from '@testing-library/react';
import Button from './Button';

describe('Button Component', () => {
  it('renders the button with the correct text', () => {
    render(<Button>Click Me</Button>);
    expect(screen.getByText('Click Me')).toBeInTheDocument();
  });

  it('calls the onClick handler when clicked', () => {
    const handleClick = jest.fn();
    render(<Button onClick={handleClick}>Click Me</Button>);
```

```
    screen.getByText('Click Me').click();
    expect(handleClick).toHaveBeenCalledTimes(1);
  });
});
```

## Testing Functions and Logic:

We'll show how to write unit tests for functions and logic within your components.

Explain how to use jest mock functions, to simulate dependencies.

## Testing Custom Hooks:

Explain how to test custom hooks, using the `@testing-library/react-hooks` library.

## 3. Writing Integration Tests with React Testing Library:

## Testing Component Interactions:

We'll demonstrate how to write integration tests to verify component interactions using React Testing Library.

Explain how to use the `fireEvent` function, to simulate user interactions.

Explain how to use the `findBy` functions, to wait for asynchronous updates.

Example:

JavaScript

```
// Counter.test.jsx
import React from 'react';
import { render, screen, fireEvent } from '@testing-library/react';
```

```
import Counter from './Counter';

describe('Counter Component', () => {
  it('increments the count when the button is clicked', () => {
    render(<Counter />);
    fireEvent.click(screen.getByText('Increment'));
    expect(screen.getByText('Count: 1')).toBeInTheDocument();
  });
});
```

## Testing[1] Asynchronous Operations:

We'll explore how to test asynchronous operations, such as API calls, using `async/await` and `waitFor`.

Explain how to use jest mock functions, to mock api calls.

## Testing Routing:

Explain how to test react router, using the `@testing-library/react-router-dom` library.

## Testing Forms:

Explain how to test forms, and form submissions.

## 4. Best Practices for Testing:

## Test-Driven Development (TDD):

We'll discuss the benefits of TDD and how to apply it to your React 19 projects.

### Writing Meaningful Tests:

We'll emphasize the importance of writing meaningful tests that cover critical functionality.

### Keeping Tests Isolated:

Explain how to keep tests isolated, to prevent them from interfering with each other.

### Using Test Doubles:

Explain how to use test doubles, like stubs, mocks, and spies.

### Code Coverage:

Explain how to use code coverage tools, to identify untested code.

### Testing Accessibility:

Explain how to test accessibility, using tools like `@testing-library/jest-dom` and `axe-core`.

### Continuous Integration (CI):

Explain how to integrate tests into a CI pipeline, to automate testing.

By mastering Jest and React Testing Library, you'll be able to write effective unit and integration tests that ensure the quality and reliability of your React 19 applications."

# 10.2 Deploying React 19 Applications to Production Environments

"Deploying your React 19 applications to production environments is the final step in making your application accessible to users. In this section, we'll explore various deployment strategies and best practices for ensuring a smooth and reliable deployment process.

## 1. Preparing for Production:

### Production Build:

We'll emphasize the importance of creating a production build of your application using `npm run build` or the equivalent for your build tool (e.g., `vite build`).

Explain how production builds are optimized for performance.

Explain how to configure your build process, for production.

### Environment Variables:

We'll discuss how to manage environment variables for production, including API keys and other sensitive information.

Explain how to use environment variables, in your hosting environment.

Explain how to use `.env.production` files.

### Performance Optimization:

We'll reiterate the importance of performance optimization before deployment, including code splitting, lazy loading, and memoization

Explain how to use performance monitoring tools, to track performance in production.

### Security Considerations:

We'll discuss security considerations, such as HTTPS, CORS, and protecting sensitive data.

Explain how to configure security headers.

## 2. Deployment Strategies:

### Static Site Hosting (Netlify, Vercel, GitHub Pages):

We'll demonstrate how to deploy static React 19 applications to platforms like Netlify, Vercel, and GitHub Pages.

Explain how to configure deployment settings.

Explain how to use continuous deployment.

Explain how to use serverless functions, with static site hosting.

### Server-Side Rendering (Node.js, Next.js):

We'll discuss how to deploy server-side rendered React 19 applications using Node.js or Next.js.

Explain how to configure a Node.js server.

Explain how to use process managers, like PM2.

Explain how to use containerization, with docker.

### Containerization (Docker, Kubernetes):

We'll explore how to containerize your React 19 applications using Docker and deploy them to platforms like Kubernetes.

Explain how to create a Dockerfile.

Explain how to use docker compose.

Explain how to use Kubernetes deployments and services.

**Cloud Platforms (AWS, Google Cloud, Azure):**

We'll discuss how to deploy React 19 applications to cloud platforms like AWS, Google Cloud, and Azure.

Explain how to use cloud services, like AWS S3, or Google Cloud Storage, for static site hosting

Explain how to use cloud services, like AWS EC2, or Google Compute Engine, for server side rendering.

Explain how to use cloud services, like AWS Elastic Beanstalk, or Google App Engine, for managed deployments.

**3. Deployment Process:**

**Continuous Integration/Continuous Deployment (CI/CD):**

We'll emphasize the importance of using CI/CD pipelines to automate the deployment process.

Explain how to use CI/CD tools, like GitHub Actions, or GitLab CI.

Explain how to automate testing, and deployment.

**Deployment Checklist:**

We'll provide a deployment checklist to ensure a smooth and reliable deployment process.

Include items like:

Test production build

Configure environment variables

Configure security settings

Monitor performance

Set up error logging

**Rollback Strategies:**

Explain how to implement rollback strategies, in case of deployment failures.

Explain how to use versioning, and how to use blue/green deployments.

**4. Monitoring and Maintenance:**

**Performance Monitoring:**

We'll discuss how to monitor the performance of your React 19 applications in production using tools like Google Analytics, or New Relic.

Explain how to track performance metrics.

**Error Logging and Monitoring:**

We'll explore how to set up error logging and monitoring using tools like Sentry or Bugsnag.

Explain how to set up alerts, for errors.

**Regular Updates and Maintenance:**

We'll emphasize the importance of regular updates and maintenance to ensure the security and performance of your applications.

Explain how to update dependencies.

Explain how to apply security patches.

### 5. Best Practices:

**Automation:**

Emphasize the importance of automating the deployment process.

**Infrastructure as Code (IaC):**

Explain the benefits of using IaC tools, like Terraform, or CloudFormation.

**Documentation:**

Explain the importance of documenting the deployment process.

**Security:**

Reiterate the importance of security in production environments.

By following these deployment strategies and best practices, you'll be able to confidently deploy your React 19 applications to production environments, ensuring a smooth and reliable user experience."

# 10.3 Maintaining Code Quality and Scalability in React 19 Projects.

"Maintaining code quality and scalability is crucial for the long-term health of your React 19 projects. This section explores strategies and best practices for ensuring your applications remain manageable and maintainable as they evolve.

### 1. Code Quality Practices:

**Code Reviews:**

We'll emphasize the importance of conducting regular code reviews to identify and address code quality issues.

Explain how to conduct effective code reviews.

Explain how to use code review tools.

## Linting and Formatting:

We'll discuss how to use linting tools (e.g., ESLint) and code formatters (e.g., Prettier) to enforce code style and catch errors.

Explain how to configure ESLint and Prettier.

Explain how to integrate linting and formatting into your CI/CD pipeline.

## Type Checking (TypeScript):

We'll advocate for using TypeScript to add static typing to your React 19 projects, improving code quality and reducing runtime errors.

Explain how to configure TypeScript.

Explain how to write type definitions

## Component Libraries and Design Systems

We'll explore how to create and maintain component libraries and design systems to promote code reuse and consistency

Explain how to use tools like Storybook, to document components.

Explain how to use tools like Bit, or Nx, to manage component libraries.

## Documentation:

We'll emphasize the importance of writing clear and comprehensive documentation for your code.

Explain how to use tools like JSDoc, or TypeDoc, to generate documentation.

Explain how to write README files, for components, and modules.

## 2. Scalability Practices:

### Modular Architecture:

We'll discuss how to adopt a modular architecture to organize your code into independent and reusable modules

Explain how to use feature-based folder structures.

Explain how to use domain-driven design principles.

### Code Splitting and Lazy Loading:

We'll reiterate the importance of code splitting and lazy loading to improve performance and reduce bundle sizes

Explain how to use dynamic imports.

Explain how to use the Suspense component.

### State Management Strategies:

We'll discuss how to choose the right state management strategy for your application, considering its complexity and scalability requirements.

Explain how to use context api, reducers, and external state management libraries.

### API Design and Communication:

We'll explore how to design efficient and scalable APIs for your React 19 applications.

Explain how to use RESTful, or GraphQL APIs.

Explain how to use api versioning.

**Performance Monitoring and Optimization:**

We'll emphasize the importance of continuously monitoring and optimizing the performance of your applications.

Explain how to use performance monitoring tools.

Explain how to use caching strategies.

**3. Refactoring and Maintenance:**

**Regular Refactoring:**

We'll advocate for conducting regular refactoring to improve code quality and address technical debt

Explain how to use refactoring patterns.

Explain how to use code analysis tools.

**Dependency Management:**

We'll discuss how to manage dependencies effectively, including updating dependencies and addressing security vulnerabilities.

Explain how to use tools like npm-check-updates, or yarn upgrade-interactive.

Explain how to use dependabot, or other dependency monitoring tools.

**Version Control (Git):**

We'll reiterate the importance of using Git for version control and collaboration.

Explain how to use branching strategies.

Explain how to use pull requests, and code reviews.

**Testing Strategies:**

We'll emphasize the importance of writing comprehensive tests to ensure code quality and prevent regressions.

Explain how to use unit tests, integration tests, and end to end tests

Explain how to use test driven development.

### 4. Team Collaboration and Communication:

**Clear Communication Channels:**

We'll discuss the importance of establishing clear communication channels for your team.

**Knowledge Sharing:**

We'll advocate for knowledge sharing through documentation, code reviews, and pair programming.

**Code Ownership and Responsibility:**

We'll discuss how to establish clear code ownership and responsibility within your team.

### 5. Continuous Improvement:

**Regular Retrospectives:**

We'll emphasize the importance of conducting regular retrospectives to identify areas for improvement.

**Staying Up-to-Date:**

We'll advocate for staying up-to-date with the latest React 19 features and best practices.

**Learning and Experimentation:**

We'll encourage a culture of learning and experimentation to foster innovation.

By implementing these code quality and scalability practices, you'll be able to maintain your React 19 projects effectively, ensuring they remain robust, manageable, and adaptable to future requirements."